MARKETPLACE DEVOTIONALS 1

31 Days
with God
at Work

JAMES **BRUYN**

Marketplace Ministry exists to raise up a new generation of leaders who understand what it means to live as a Christian in the Marketplace. Marketplace Ministry equips women and men to courageously explain how their faith in God relates to their work and impacts their relationships with co-workers.

For more information, visit www.marketplace-ministry.ca

31 Days with God at Work

Copyright © 2018 James Bruyn

ISBN 978-1-77538-050-4 (softcover)
ISBN 978-1-77538-051-1 (e-book)

All rights reserved. No part of this book may be reproduced in any form, except for brief quotations in printed reviews, without permission in writing from the author.

Unless otherwise noted, all Scripture quotations are taken from THE HOLY BIBLE, NEW INTERNATIONAL VERSION®, NIV® Copyright © 1973, 1978, 1984, 2011 by Biblica, Inc.® Used by permission. All rights reserved worldwide. Scripture quotations marked NKJV are taken from the New King James Version®. Copyright © 1982 by Thomas Nelson. Used by permission. All rights reserved. Scripture quotations marked THE MESSAGE are taken from THE MESSAGE. Copyright © by Eugene H. Peterson 1993, 2002. Used by permission of Tyndale House Publishers, Inc. Scripture quotations marked NET are taken from NET Bible® copyright ©1996-2006 by Biblical Studies Press, L.L.C. http://netbible.com All rights reserved. The names: THE NET BIBLE®, NEW ENGLISH TRANSLATION COPYRIGHT © 1996 BY BIBLICAL STUDIES PRESS, L.L.C. NET Bible® IS A REGISTERED TRADEMARK THE NET BIBLE® LOGO, SERVICE MARK COPYRIGHT © 1997 BY BIBLICAL STUDIES PRESS, L.L.C. ALL RIGHTS RESERVED.

Editor: Erin/WriteEditor.net
Cover and interior design and typeset: Katherine/theDESKonline.com
Cover image: Rawpixel/istockphoto

CONTENTS

Introduction	Workday Prayer	1
Day 1	Wisdom for the Workplace	3
Day 2	A Project of Daring Faith	5
Day 3	Demonstrating the Existence of God's Kingdom!	7
Day 4	Bridging Two Worlds	9
Day 5	A Larger Reality	11
Day 6	God Is with You	13
Day 7	Job Satisfaction	15
Day 8	God Delights over You	18
Day 9	Creation	20
Day 10	God Gives Grace to the Humble	22
Day 11	Stressful Workdays	24
Day 12	Is Doubt Crowding Out Hope?	26
Day 13	I Find No Fault in You	28
Day 14	Walking with God	30
Day 15	Look to Jesus	32
Day 16	Calling	34
Day 17	Who Is Your Neighbor?	36
Day 18	A Canopy of Grace	38
Day 19	Preparing for the Future	40
Day 20	God Is Watching over You	42
Day 21	Why Are You Afraid?	44

Day 22	God's Presence	46
Day 23	Working with Integrity	48
Day 24	An Oasis of Grace	50
Day 25	The Way of Righteousness	52
Day 26	Courage	54
Day 27	Stewards of God's Creation	57
Day 28	No Little Tasks	59
Day 29	Can God Fix It?	61
Day 30	Thriving in Your Workplace	64
Day 31	Abiding in Christ in the Workplace	67

About the Author 71

Also by the Author 73

INTRODUCTION

Workday Prayer

*And whatever you do, whether in word or deed,
do it all in the name of the Lord Jesus,
giving thanks to God the Father through him.*

COLOSSIANS 3:17

Father in Heaven,
Thank you that I can rest in your holy presence through the shed blood of your Son. May my life and work honor your holy name. Help me to keep my eyes focused on you and your kingdom as I go about my work.

May my work, my attitudes, and my speech be pleasing in your sight and be in accordance with your will. May everything that my employer and colleagues do and say be in accordance with your will.

Thank you for giving me the skills, energy, and creativity to earn my daily bread. Thank you for this job and employer, which provide for my daily bread.

Forgive me when my actions or attitudes or words are not pleasing to you. Fill me with your love for my coworkers and customers so that I am able to forgive.

Keep me from temptation at work so that I might not sin before your holy presence. Deliver me from people and situations that wish to harm me or bring evil into my life.

Enable me to be a bearer of grace, hope, joy, and peace, even in the most stressful of situations. May I go about my work in such a way that my coworkers and customers glorify your holy name.

Amen.

DAY 1

Wisdom for the Workplace

Wisdom calls aloud outside;
She raises her voice in the open squares.
She cries out in the chief concourses,
At the openings of the gates in the city
She speaks her words.
PROVERBS 1:20–21

At your place of work, in the midst of all the noise competing for your heart's attention, God calls to you, offering you his wisdom. God's wisdom is unique. This world in which you live and work is God's handiwork. As the Creator, God is the only one who knows exactly how everything is designed. Instead of providing you with an owner's manual, the Creator desires to enter into a personal relationship with you and to share firsthand how everything functions. Relying on his wisdom and understanding will enable you to do your job with excellence.

God's wisdom is true, just, and perfect. It will teach you prudence and discretion and provide you with counsel and sound judgment and insight. God's wisdom will enable you to make just decisions and to lead well. God understands the intricacies of the hearts of those you work and live alongside, so with his wisdom you can love and relate to them in a way that aligns with God's kingdom purposes.

The wisdom of God comes with a promise of a rich blessing. Should you choose to follow his wisdom, your life will produce fruit that is more precious than rubies and better than fine gold, and its yield surpasses choice silver. The day is coming when Christ will redeem the work you are doing today. If you are going about your work with God's wisdom, no matter how menial or fascinating the work is, when it is refined by fire, in some inexplicable, mysterious way, it will be purified as gold and silver.

The work you are doing today has immense value when you continually rely on God's wisdom. The One who created you, rejoices over you, and loves you says this to you today:

> So now, children, listen to me;
> blessed are those who keep my ways.
> Listen to my instruction so that you may be wise,
> and do not neglect it.
> Blessed is the one who listens to me,
> watching at my doors day by day,
> waiting beside my doorway.
> For the one who finds me finds life
> and receives favor from the Lord.
> (Proverbs 8:33–35 NET)

PRAYER

Almighty God, give me ears to hear your words of instruction so that I may always dwell in your house and bring glory to your name by the way I live. *Amen.*

DAY 2

A Project of Daring Faith

Press on toward the goal to win the prize for which God has called you heavenward in Christ Jesus.

PHILIPPIANS 3:14

A life anchored in faith, living as a citizen of heaven, sets you free to enjoy everything this world that God's created has to offer. As a person of faith, you can live here and now to the max. With your faith grounded in God's kingdom, as an employee, a manager, or an executive; as a parent or a spouse; as a friend or a student, you have the privilege of enriching the lives of those around you.

In Genesis 12 God appears to Abraham and gives him a call and a promise—a call to follow God to a land that he would show Abraham, and a promise to bless Abraham and to make him a blessing.

Abraham chose to obey God, leaving behind the "seen" world of his former days and launching into a project of "daring faith." He believed that the riches of God's kingdom immeasurably surpassed anything this world had to offer. Abraham kept his focus on heaven—a city whose foundations God designed and built.

When Abraham arrived in the land God led him to, by faith

he made a reality of what wasn't obvious to an onlooker: he farmed, raised sheep, and dug wells. He was financially rewarded for his hard labor. At the same time, the people he lived among came to respect him as a Prince of God (Gen. 23:6). They viewed him as a ruler, and he went so far as to go into battle to free the kings of that area. Abraham's servants (we would call them employees today) acknowledged that God was the source of Abraham's blessings (Gen. 24:27).

While he enjoyed the wealth and prestige he earned by his labor, people knew that Abraham's life rested on the stability of the promises of God, not on material things. By going in faith where God sent him, Abraham brought glory to God. Abraham's hard work and leadership among the people where he lived honored God. Abraham worshipped God by his faithful obedience throughout his life. Therefore, God was not ashamed to be called the God of Abraham. He counted Abraham as a righteous man.

When people observe your life, what do they see? Do they see your abilities, do they see your wealth, or do they see your faith in God?

PRAYER

Almighty God, who has prepared good works for each of us to do, give me the courage to choose to launch into the project of daring faith that you have called me to so that your name would be honored and glorified through Jesus Christ our Lord, *Amen.*

DAY 3

Demonstrating the Existence of God's Kingdom!

*I will rejoice in the Lord,
I will be joyful in God my Savior.*
HABAKKUK 3:18

As you look beyond what is happening today in your life and obediently believe in the future God promised, you are demonstrating the existence of God's kingdom to your coworkers. In the midst of the daily routine of life, your songs of praise and thanksgiving demonstrate to a watching world that our God reigns.

You show that God's kingdom exists when you allow God to lead you moment by moment and in every situation. Your life is a testimony to God when you lovingly obey God, staying where he tells you to stay, going where he sends you to go, doing what he tells you to do, speaking what he tells you to say, and remaining silent when he tells you to be silent.

When your love never gives up on someone, when you never lose faith, when you are always hopeful, when you endure through difficult and joyful circumstances, no one can doubt that God is real.

The truth of God's kingdom cannot be denied when people see the fruit of God's Spirit in your life—love, joy, peace, patience, kindness, goodness, gentleness, and self-control. At those times when you catch yourself being conceited, provocative, envious, selfish, lusting, boastful, proud, hateful, impatient, lazy, unkind, or angered and you seek forgiveness from the person you have sinned against and accept God's gracious unconditional forgiveness, you proclaim to a watching world that a gracious, merciful, loving heavenly Father exists.

This isn't easy. Your finite, logical mind often can't make sense of what God is doing. It's challenging because you rarely understand God's timing. It doesn't help when people bully, ridicule, or mock you for believing something that cannot be seen.

What keeps you going at these times is a quiet confidence that a loving God who created this world out of nothing is faithful to his promises and will accomplish what you cannot see. When you have doubts and fears, admit them and ask God to help you look past them so that you can see his love and holiness.

How does your attitude and behavior demonstrate to your coworkers that the kingdom of God exists?

PRAYER

Almighty God, who has seated us with Christ in the heavenly realms, help me to go about my work today in a manner that is pleasing to your sight so that the world may know that your kingdom exists. *Amen.*

DAY 4

Bridging Two Worlds

*Seek first God's kingdom and God's righteousness,
and all these things will be given to you as well.*
MATTHEW 6:33–34

At your workplace your life is intertwined with the real stories, hurts, experiences, fears, successes, and failures of your coworkers. At the same time, your life is immersed in the Scriptures, living and inhaling the love, hope, and grace of Christ. How do you connect these two kingdoms? Or are they two separate worlds?

Bridging these worlds starts as you trust in the solid rock of your loving heavenly Father without wavering. When you are wholeheartedly seeking God, his joy washes away the anxiety in your heart. A life without anxiety is a contagious life.

Bridging these worlds occurs as you interact with people. Doing your work with excellence and constantly learning and improving your skills will earn you the right to be heard and respected. It is in your relationships with people that you exhale the love, hope, and grace of God.

You can connect these two worlds by seeking God and his righteousness in the midst of all the stories your life intertwines with. God is able to provide you with wisdom so that your righteousness shines brightly in your conversations and conduct so that Christ in you, the hope of glory, is revealed.

Seeking God's righteousness requires a constant and careful examination of your life so that you guard yourself against sin. This includes the sins of judging others and focusing on their faults rather than allowing the Holy Spirit to transform your life into Christ's image. An attitude of seeking God's righteousness involves forgiving others even as you have been forgiven. Christ is willing to forgive you and forgive your coworkers.

In quiet confidence with your head held high and with a holy faith, knowing that you are secure in your Father's hand, passionately ask, seek, and knock at the throne room of heaven on behalf of the real stories of your colleagues. Ask, seek, and knock until they receive with gratitude God's precious gifts, until they are transformed by Christ, until they open the door and enter by faith into God's kingdom.

PRAYER

Almighty Father, who in your great love and rich mercy has made us alive in Christ, you know the stories of my colleagues. Work a miracle in their lives so that they might glorify your holy name. *Amen.*

DAY 5

A Larger Reality

Do you not know? Have you not heard?
The Lord is the everlasting God, the Creator of the ends
of the earth. He will not grow tired or weary, and his
understanding no one can fathom.

ISAIAH 40:28

God is intimately present with his inexhaustible power and love in all of his creation at all times, including your workplace. God is not limited by time and space. He knows every truth about his creation, even those that we haven't discovered yet. While constant change is happening around you, his moral principles, his attributes, his purposes, his motives, his promises, and his love for you never change.

This world is established, firm, and secure because the Lord, robed in majesty, is in complete control and is exalted above all his creation. Your workplace exists between the boundaries of the waters that God held in the hollow of his hand and the mountains and hills that God weighed on the scales (Isa. 40:12).

Every task you do at work takes place in God's creation. The tools you use for your work were shaped from raw materials that God created. The principles that govern your work are principles that God established when he created the universe. The systems that bring structure to your work are systems that are rooted in the very nature of God's creation.

God's authority is ruling over everything that happens at your company. God is ruling in accordance with his loving, unchanging, unsearchable wisdom, which is deeper and richer than you will ever grasp. God created the thrones, powers, and systems of this world.

As the sovereign Lord, God has appointed the times and places in history for each person. In his unsearchable wisdom, God knows what he is doing when he places people in leadership over us at work and in government. There is great freedom in recognizing that God has marked out the appointed time in history and boundaries of those around us. We may not understand why God has placed certain people in certain roles, but the good news is we don't need to. God understands and asks us to trust in his infinite wisdom.

The Lord, armed with strength, is in control of every aspect of your workplace. God, who created the heavens and the earth, knows how to deal with the deadlines, pressures, power struggles, stressors, and frustrations you face in your workplace.

PRAYER

Almighty God, creator of heaven and earth, give me a glimpse of your power and glory in my work today so that I may worship you in all of your majesty. *Amen.*

DAY 6

God Is with You

*The virgin will conceive and give birth to a son,
and they will call him Immanuel
(which means "God with us").*

MATTHEW 1:23

God is with you! God is with you today in your workplace. God hears each conversation. God knows what people are thinking about you and your work. God is with you while you perform each task of your job. No matter how mundane your work may be, when you are in continual communion with God, your work is sacred.

Start your workday with God at your side. Enjoy the immense privilege of God being with you right now. As you begin each task, or before each interaction with people, in your spirit, freely call out "Abba, Father" and know that God hears you.

Who is with you today at work? The Lord of heaven and earth is with you! The God of peace, grace, truth, and light is with you. The loving, holy, and righteous God is your constant companion. God delights over you with his whole being. God hears your prayers and is providing the wisdom you need for this moment.

Allow God's presence to fill you with joy! Be strong and courageous! God is with you! God will never leave you nor forsake you!

With God at your right hand, you can live a grace-filled life without shame, seeking no reward, fearing nothing, being afraid of no one. Seek God so that you can go about your work with boldness, joy, love, power, and gratitude. Freely give. Freely forgive. Freely love. Enjoy each moment at work, basking in God's presence.

PRAYER

Almighty God, you have promised never to leave me or forsake me. Today I need your presence with me in my workplace so that I might reflect your joy and peace. *Amen.*

DAY 7

Job Satisfaction

> *Trust in the Lord with all your heart
> and lean not on your own understanding.*
>
> PROVERBS 3:5

God created you as a unique, whole, infinitely complex individual. Your primary skills and your unique personality enable you to make distinct and meaningful contributions to your employer. You have many other minor gifts and talents that enable you to do your job slightly different from anybody else.

If you are thoroughly enjoying your work today, pause to give thanks to God for all his blessings. Rejoice that God has given you the skills that you use in your job. Celebrate that God has placed you in a role where you can use your skills and abilities.

If you experience twinges of dissatisfaction or unrest in your current role, rejoice! Rejoice that God has created you with infinitely more facets than others recognize. Maybe you don't realize them yourself. Prayerfully consider how you might use these talents and attributes within the constraints of your position at work, with the goal of maximizing your value to your employer. If you are a manager, look for qualities in your team beyond what you hired them for. Find creative ways to allow your staff to use their talents and to express their complex beauty.

Sometimes you may find yourself in a job where you believe your value is not fully appreciated. Maybe you may think you are able to contribute more to the organization, or possibly you feel that you would be more fulfilled if you were to use your skills in a different role. When you focus your attention and energy on the apparent injustice or inequality of your situation, it is easy to become negative and lose sight of God. If that is the way you feel today, I invite you to step back for a moment, to abandon the illusion that you are in control of this world, and to reflect on God's character. Does God change when you feel like you are a square peg in a round hole? Does God's love for you, your hope, or your salvation disappear when you feel like your skills are being underutilized? Did God make a mistake when he placed you in this position? Is this situation beyond God's redemptive power? Can you trust that this job, for right now, is part of God's perfect plan for your life?

Whether you feel like your current job is a great fit for who you are, or your job situation is less than ideal, continue to trust in the love and care of your heavenly Father. God says to you, "My child, trust me. I am sovereign. I am in control. I love you. I have placed these people in authority over you; I have appointed their times and boundaries, and all because I love you." Make it your goal to please God. Give thanks to the Lord that you have been granted the privilege to participate in what God is doing in your workplace.

What would it take to say, "I have learned to be content in my current job"? What does it look like for you to trust in God as you go about your work?

Regarding your workplace situation, can you identify with one biblical character who experienced something similar (e.g., Joseph)? Reread his or her story. How does this example inspire you?

PRAYER

Almighty God, who has blessed me with the skills and abilities to make a unique contribution to your world, forgive me for my lack of gratitude and help me to go about my work in such a way that your name is honored. *Amen.*

DAY 8

God Delights over You

> *The Lord your God in your midst,*
> *The Mighty One, will save;*
> *He will rejoice over you with gladness,*
> *He will quiet you with His love,*
> *He will rejoice over you with singing.*
>
> ZEPHANIAH 3:17

God delights over you! God rejoices over you! Each facet of your life wonderfully reflects his glory. His love sparkles as you apply to your job your spiritual gifts and the talents and skills he gave you.

Each of your abilities is a precious gift God uniquely chose for you for his honor and glory before you were born. Your abilities and talents are not to be despised or abused. They are just as important as your spiritual gifts. God has filled you with the wisdom, the knowledge, and the understanding to use your talents and abilities.

In the Old Testament, we meet leaders like Moses, Joseph, and Gideon who were filled with the Spirit of God as well as wisdom, knowledge, and understanding. We also read about talented tradespeople whom God filled with wisdom, knowledge, and understanding to build the tabernacle and its furnishings, sew the priests' garments, farm, raise cattle, herd sheep, and do countless other jobs.

Wisdom, knowledge, and understanding are part of the essence of God's character. He used these to create this world. God has blessed you with the wisdom to learn and to teach others the skills you use to do your job with excellence. God has blessed you with the knowledge to do what is necessary to fulfill the requirements of your job. God has blessed you with understanding to solve the inevitable problems that arise in your job.

May you do your work in a manner worthy of the Lord, who has blessed you with wisdom, knowledge, and understanding. May you please the Lord in every way as you go about your job. May every good work you do bear fruit.

Continue to grow in the knowledge of God. Be the best you that you can be in your workplace to the honor and glory of God! That is how God has gifted you, how God has created you, and who God has called you to be!

PRAYER

Almighty God, I praise you for the wisdom, knowledge, and understanding you have blessed me with. Help me to go about my work in manner that is pleasing in your eyes so that your name would be glorified. *Amen.*

DAY 9

Creation

*All things were made through Him,
and without Him nothing was made that was made.*
JOHN 1:3

God created this universe, including all its natural resources. God blessed individuals with skills and gifts to shape these raw materials into the things we use and enjoy. The laws of nature, which you rely upon to design and build everything you have, were established by the Lord of heaven and earth when he created the universe. Receive what you have and what you use today with thanksgiving.

There are no little jobs and no little people in God's kingdom. Every role is vitally important. Architects and engineers design a building using the principles of engineering that are inherent in the world God created. Construction crews use the natural resources that God created to build a new building. Accountants bring order to the finances of a building project, just as God brought order into the universe he created. Equally important are the baristas who serve coffee, derived from coffee plants originally planted by God in the garden, to the architects, engineers, accountants, and construction crew.

Doing your work fulfills the mandate that God gave each of us in Genesis to fill the earth and to be responsible for it. As you

CREATION

go about your job today, acknowledge that God is the Creator and Lord of all the things you have. When celebrating the privilege to use what God created, you not only discover and follow the principles of God's world, you also are constantly reminding those around you that this is our Father's world and not a random collection of particles.

PRAYER

Almighty God, I thank you for your creation and blessings. Forgive me when I take things for granted. Help me to live in such a way that my friends, neighbors, and coworkers will understand that this is your world. *Amen.*

DAY 10

God Gives Grace to the Humble

*God resists the proud,
But gives grace to the humble.*
JAMES 4:6

When you look back over your career, when you consider all the things you have accomplished, when you remember all your possessions (even if they are few), may your heart be filled with humble praise and adoration to the Lord for his goodness to you.

All these things are blessings from the hand of the Lord. Your very existence is a blessing from God. The skills and talents you used throughout your career to achieve your accomplishments are gifts from God. The managers, teachers, and colleagues who helped you along the way are blessings from him. It is only through the grace of God and his sustaining presence in your life and this universe that you are able to read this devotional.

It's true that many people believe they have gotten where they are in their careers because of a combination of luck, hard work, and self-sufficiency. They believe that they are the masters of their own universes. They came and they conquered. They think that they are without peer, that they are self-sufficient. They worship

God Gives Grace to the Humble

themselves and expect others to worship them as well. In their arrogance, they live blindfolded in a world of illusion, cut off from the life of God through ignorance and insensitivity. Out of his infinite mercy and grace, God invites them to repent and acknowledge that all their blessings come from Him.

Don't let yourself be distracted by these people. Instead, keep your eyes focused on your loving heavenly Father! Remember that God opposes the proud and gives grace to the humble.

Give thanks to God from a grateful heart for all he has done for you.

PRAYER

Gracious Father, I am humbled that you are mindful of me, a mere creature of dust. Forgive me for my pride. Help me never to forget the source of my blessings. *Amen.*

DAY 11

Stressful Workdays

A bruised reed he will not break,
and a smoldering wick he will not snuff out.
Isaiah 42:3

Stressful workdays. Days when the boss drops three piles of work onto your desk just as you are ready to go home, and he demands that it be ready for the next morning. Days when your computer dies and you have fifteen minutes left to finish your presentation. Days when the best you can do is shake your head in wonder at the way your managers, customers, or coworkers are behaving. Days when it feels like you, or everybody in your company, got out of the wrong side of bed. Days filled with stress when everything around you cries out in denial of God.

Jesus in his righteousness will meet you in your stress today. He has taken the broken places where you work and the broken pieces of your life and is raising them to new life, giving them new meaning and giving you purpose. In Christ this is not a psychological possibility but a present reality. Because of Jesus' infinite grace, righteousness, and redemptive power of forgiveness, you are growing into a mature, compassionate, and wise leader. Praise the Lord!

Jesus delights in your continued faithfulness in your workplace. He weeps over your struggle to cope with yet another

Stressful Workdays

tough, stressful workday. Jesus continues to strengthen you so that you don't grow weary as you faithfully, prayerfully, even tearfully prepare to go back to work again tomorrow and the next day, and the day after that.

Jesus sees your faithfulness, your deeds, your hard work, and your perseverance. He sees your continual demonstration of his love in your workplace. Jesus knows that you have remained true to his holy name and not walked away from your faith. The One who is holy and true knows that though you are weak, you faithfully depend on his strength. Continue to buy from God gold refined in the fire so that you build up treasures in heaven.

Allow Christ to keep cleansing you from all unrighteousness so that you may wear clothes washed whiter than snow. Allow Jesus to touch your eyes so that you might see him. Continue to be faithful, and one day Christ will crown you with the victor's crown and grant you the right to eat from the Tree of Life, which is in the paradise of God. The day is coming when you will reign with him in glory forever.

PRAYER

Almighty God, I praise you that you reward me for my faithfulness and not my feelings. I am weak and I need your strength today so that my life may bring glory and honor to your name. *Amen.*

DAY 12

Is Doubt Crowding Out Hope?

*This hope we have as an anchor of the soul,
both sure and steadfast.*
HEBREWS 6:19

At the intersection of spiritual life and vocation are two signs. One sign is marked doubt: "God's promises are in jeopardy. Put your hope in your own abilities, and take matters in your own hands." The other sign is marked hope: "God is bound to his word by his character. Put your hope in God and obey with unwavering confidence."

Satan urges you to lean on your own understanding and follow the path of doubt. Jesus invites you to choose hope, to trust him with all your heart, and to submit all your ways to him. Doubt invites you to be wise in your own eyes. Hope calls you to fear the Lord and shun evil. Hope is the antidote to shame, for hope in God will never disappoint you. Hope enables you to joyfully allow God to take you forward into maturity.

One would think that hope would grow in the quiet places, or in the holy of holies at God's throne of grace. But hope grows in the messy, sinful world. Hope grows as you engage with culture and see the wonderful power of Christ in operation. Hope grows

Is Doubt Crowding Out Hope?

as you practice living out righteousness. Hope grows as you experience the reality that God's promises are absolutely trustworthy in every moment and in every season of life.

Doubt is a slippery slope leading to death. It is filled with devious behavior, deceit, seduction, and evil. The path of hope is a good path, a straight path, the path of life marked by love and faithfulness. Along the path of hope you will find abundant wisdom and sufficient understanding to prudently make the next choice in your vocation.

With hope by your side, your walk will be blameless, and God will be your shield, for he guards the course of the just and protects the way of his faithful ones (Prov. 2:7–8). When you choose the way of hope, you live in eternal safety, and your soul will be at ease without fear of harm (Prov. 1:33). Living with hope, you have no need to fear the disaster or ruin that will one day overtake the wicked. Along the path of hope, the Lord is at your side, keeping your foot from being caught in the snare of sins. With hope you can run and not grow weary.

PRAYER

Almighty God, thank you that my hope in you can be an anchor for my soul. Remind me today of the hope that I have in you so that I am not discouraged. *Amen*

DAY 13

I Find No Fault in You

Neither do I condemn you; go and sin no more.
JOHN 8:11

When you hear the name Gideon or Samson, what is the first thing that comes to your mind? Is it Gideon's fleece, or Samson's Delilah? It is interesting that when we think of people, we often think of their colorful faults or weaknesses. The author of Hebrews reminds us that when God sees Gideon or Samson, he doesn't see someone who is frightened or interested in women. Rather, God remembers their faith!

Do not let your faults discourage you. Do not believe Satan when he tells you that you are unworthy when your faith fails at times. In each one us, something sinful can be found. My faith is halting and imperfect many times. However, none of that changes how God sees me. God sees us as men and women of faith.

When your faith falters, when your faith is imperfect and incomplete, Jesus intercedes on your behalf to God, his Father and your Father. Jesus says, "I died for their imperfections and faltering faith." And with great joy God says, "Yes! Because I raised you, Jesus, my Son, from the dead, I find no fault in these my precious children!"

I Find No Fault in You

Hear the words that God says to you today: "I find no fault in you!"

Do not be discouraged. Press on in faith!

God sees Gideon, Samson, David, and you as living stories of his power. Your story renews confidence to your friends, coworkers, and family, even to future generations to receive God's grace and forgiveness.

Since God sees no fault in you, in faith fulfill the calling God has placed in your heart. Continue to be a faithful husband or wife, son or daughter! Continue to be a faithful worker, manager, student, entrepreneur—whatever God has called you to be.

May many people be inspired as your life story demonstrates God's ability to turn weakness into strength and to deliver in times of need!

PRAYER

Almighty God, thank you that I can stand blameless and righteous in your presence through the cleansing blood of your Son who died for me. I need you today to deliver me from the evil one so that my life might be pleasing in your sight. *Amen.*

DAY 14

Walking with God

Without faith it is impossible to please God, because anyone who comes to him must believe that he exists and that he rewards those who earnestly seek him.

HEBREWS 11:6

God eagerly desires for you to walk with him. It doesn't matter what you are wearing, who you are, or what you have done. It doesn't matter who are your friends or coworkers. The joyous privilege of enjoying intimacy with God rests solely on his grace.

When you walk with God, he doesn't run ahead then jump out from behind a tree to scare you. When you walk with God, he doesn't race off and disappear into traffic. *Yahweh*, the One who delivers on his promises, stays by your side so that you can continuously look full on his wonderful face in every activity of your day.

God won't hurt you, stomp on you, crush you, or say things against you when you are hurting. Instead, the Good Shepherd will tenderly lift you up and carry you in his arms. The author of life and light won't extinguish the spark of life and light inside you. Rather, he will fan the flame so that your light will shine more brightly.

As you enjoy fellowship with God, you will learn his vocabulary of sin and grace. As you take the first step of faith with him, he will continue to turn your heart toward himself, and he will teach you how to keep his commands in all you say and do.

Even in the midst of a world that does not know peace or joy, when you walk with God, you enter into a warm, prayerful, worshipping relationship with the Lord of the universe.

When you walk with God, you bring light into the darkest of rooms. When you are in fellowship with God, you bring the sweet fragrance of God's peace and joy into the lives of those around you. But even better than that, God is pleased with your faith!

You have the privilege of walking with God, the One whose image you bear, the One who loves you more than you can imagine, the One who created this world you live in.

What is holding you back from accepting God's invitation to walk with him? Why are you afraid to do or say what God wants you to do or say? Is that part of your life that you want to hang onto better than what God offers you?

PRAYER

Almighty God, I am humbled that you who knows all my weaknesses would still choose to walk beside me. Help me to shine your light brightly in every situation so that you would be honored. *Amen.*

DAY 15

Look to Jesus

*What we do see is Jesus, made
"not quite as high as angels," and then,
through the experience of death, crowned so much higher
than any angel, with a glory "bright with Eden's dawn light."*

Hebrews 2:9 (The Message)

In the middle of your life and work, focus on Jesus, the pioneer of your salvation who was made perfect by what he suffered. When God created humankind, he crowned us with glory and honor and subjected creation to us. However, after the fall, we lost that position. Because of the fall, Jesus took on human form and suffered a horrible death in order to purchase our salvation. Now we see Jesus crowned with glory and honor. As you look at Jesus, the One who set you free from the bondage of sin and the fear of death, he will show you a brighter and bigger future filled with hope.

Jesus assures you that a day is coming when he will establish a new heaven and a new earth, God's kingdom, in which workplaces, communities, and even the world will be what they were meant to be. Together with Jesus you will reign in God's kingdom. With joy and delight Jesus brought you to glory, to the throne room of heaven, and introduced you as one of the children God gave him. Jesus is not ashamed to call you his brother or sister.

Look to Jesus

Jesus fully understands the temptations you face, for he shared in our humanity. Keep your eyes focused on Jesus, for he is able to help you when you face temptations at work. Jesus worked as a carpenter and knows what it is like for tools to be dull or misplaced.

Jesus interacted with the best and worst of people. He led a group of disciples and experienced all the challenges and disappointments of friendships and betrayals, of followers and saboteurs. Look to Jesus, for he is merciful. He empathizes with you in your sufferings and trials because he experienced them all. Look to Jesus as your example, for he was faithful and endured to the end.

When you look to Jesus, you can walk through this day with hope, knowing that your life can be lived as it was meant to be lived—fully alive in God's presence.

PRAYER

Almighty God, I thank you that your Son has experienced all the things that I experience in my life and can relate to my struggles. Father, deliver me from the temptations I face at work today so that your joy may be full. *Amen.*

DAY 16

Calling

> *"I am the Lord's servant," Mary answered.*
> *"May your word to me be fulfilled."*
> LUKE 1:38

God is calling you today, maybe to a role that is exciting or to a place that the world deems ordinary. That is not important. What is important is that God is calling you to be exactly who he created you to be when he knit you in your mother's womb. When God created you, he knew when and where the world needed you and your unique gifts and skills. He knew that only you could accomplish what needed to be done in this world.

God is calling you today to a life of quiet obedience and faithful trust in every situation, in every conversation, in the good times and the bad. He is calling you today to use the skills and talents he blessed you with right where you are. God's call on your life is tremendously freeing, for his call on your life is for you to be you.

You don't have to be afraid. The One who calls you today sees exactly what is occurring in this world, and he is grieved by the sinfulness he sees. His heart longs for redemption and reconciliation, but he is not surprised or panicking. What a privilege you have to constantly enjoy the presence of the One who called you, who is in control of this universe as you take the next step in obedience. No matter how many scary, dark, wonderful, or joyous situations you experience, God promises to be with you and never to leave you alone or forsake you. When you are tempted to say, "What if this happens?" or "What if that doesn't happen?" or when you doubt your ability to follow his call, what are you saying about God and who he created you to be?

God has given sufficient guidance for you to step into your calling. His Word is a lamp lighting your way. God blessed you with everything you need (people, gifts, resources, skills) to faithfully move forward. The One who calls you is your Creator. He is aware of your weaknesses and limitations, whether physical, emotional, financial, or whatever. God is calling you because he knows that your unique combination of strengths and weaknesses are exactly what is required to fulfill the task he wants you to do.

It is never too late to start being the person God created you to be. Be obedient today and faithfully follow what you know about God. Nothing is stopping you from trusting God. God is with you. God will deliver you. God is faithful and will keep his promises toward you. Even though nobody around you may be trusting God, you can! Today model Christ's love! Today you can model grace!

PRAYER

Almighty God, help me to run with perseverance the race marked out for me, fixing my eyes on your Son, Jesus, the pioneer and perfecter of faith. *Amen.*

DAY 17

Who Is Your Neighbor?

We love because he first loved us.
1 John 4:19

Do you ever ask, "Who is my neighbor?" Neighbors come from surprising places. Your neighbor is different from my neighbor. Neighbors can be down the street, in the office, on the team, or halfway across the world. Neighbors can be the same ethnicity as you, or not. Neighbors might support different political parties. Whoever your neighbors may be, they are people created in the image of God, people like you, with hopes and dreams; people who need to know that they are precious, that they are important, and that they are loved.

Are your neighbors only those people who are your friendly customers, or the outgoing coworkers who go the extra mile to make your job and the workplace a fun place to work? Do your neighbors include colleagues who live paycheck to paycheck, wondering if they are next on the lay-off list? Is the new employee who is struggling to learn the ropes and do his job or the employee who is creating more work for you also your neighbor? Is your supervisor your neighbor?

Out of love for the Lord your God, when you see that person

Who Is Your Neighbor?

who desperately needs a neighbor, choose to love him or her as yourself, even as Christ first loved you. You have been filled with the Holy Spirit, the Comforter who will guide you into all truth and wisdom so that you can discern who your neighbors are and how best to love them. As you rest in your Father's love, you will find the strength today, this moment, to love your coworkers. If you ask him, he gives you the grace to hear their hearts, hopes, and dreams. Truly, you can love your neighbors because Christ first loved you.

PRAYER

> Almighty God, thank you for your great love for me. You ask me to love others as I love myself. I cannot do this on my own strength, so I ask you to walk beside me and fill me with your love for my coworkers, for those who desperately need a neighbor. *Amen.*

DAY 18

A Canopy of Grace

When the righteous prosper, the city rejoices;
Through the blessing of the upright a city is exalted.
PROVERBS 11:10A, 11A

Your righteousness is making a difference in your workplace. Your godly behavior is bringing a blessing to the people where you work. Your honesty is noticed not only by your employer but by the people you work with. Because you don't make excuses but do your assigned work well and with a smile, you are appreciated. Your attention to the little things like going the extra mile to make sure that the tools and supplies in your workplace are in the right order so that work is easier for your colleagues hasn't gone unnoticed.

Many people find it remarkable that you quietly avoid joining your coworkers to gripe about your boss or complain about the way management runs the company. In fact, when people ask your opinion, they are amazed that you always say something positive. When you speak, people know that you are speaking the truth motivated by love, with a desire to see things improve, rather than to belittle or hurt others. In fact, nobody can remember you ever stabbing somebody in the back or saying hateful things.

Your righteous behavior is making a difference in your organization. Within your sphere of influence (however limited that might be), by being Christ's living presence in your workplace, by having the Lord's favor rest upon you, you are a "canopy of grace" for your coworkers. Your words, your smiles, your peaceful demeanor bring joy and gladness to people's hearts. Because you delight in the law of the Lord, God planted you like a tree that brings a cool shadow of protection and beauty within your workplace.

The Lord promised that as you continue to trust in him with all your heart, he will make your paths straight. He didn't say that your paths will be easy, but he promised that wherever your path leads, he will be with you, his Word will light your way, he will delight over you, and he will bring blessings through you to those around you. Wherever you go, by your righteousness, faith in your living Savior, and obedience to your risen Lord, you bring a canopy of grace to those in your sphere of influence.

PRAYER

Almighty God, may the meditations of my heart, the words from my mouth, and the work of my hands be pleasing in your sight. *Amen.*

DAY 19

Preparing for the Future

*My grace is sufficient for you,
for my power is made perfect in weakness.*
2 Corinthians 12:9a

God has brought you to this point in your life. He is fully aware of what was happening in the world and in your life as you grew up. God knows the joys and heartaches you've experienced. He has been with you every step of your life, blessing you with wisdom, understanding, and knowledge. He has brought you to this present stage in your life.

God says to you today, "My child, I love you. I am with you! I know what is going on. I am in control. My grace is sufficient for you today. Enjoy the blessings of this moment!"

As you prepare for tomorrow, you have no need to be afraid, for God brought you to this place and time, and he promised never to leave you or forsake you. Continue to seek God, his kingdom, and his righteousness. Embrace his commands. Trust in his goodness. When tomorrow comes, God will provide you with the strength to face the new day.

Whatever happens next in your life is totally under God's control and is not a surprise to him. He blessed you with the talents and skills to handle each new situation. As new situations and challenges arise, he will not allow you to be tempted beyond what you are able. God is preparing you right now for what is next in your life.

What do you need to do to prepare for tomorrow? Are there things you need to stop doing, are there things you need to get rid of, are there new skills you need to learn, or are there people you need to talk to?

PRAYER

Almighty God, thank you that you have been with me every day of my life. Forgive me for those things that have crept into my life that keep me from worshipping you. Thank you for the wonderful, diverse group of people you have surrounded me with, and the unique gifts you have given each one of them. Lord, I place my future in your hands. Give me the wisdom to use my time today wisely as I prepare for tomorrow. *Amen.*

DAY 20

God Is Watching over You

For the eyes of the Lord range throughout the earth to strengthen those whose hearts are fully committed to him.

2 Chronicles 16:9

As you arose from your bed this morning, the eyes of the Lord were watching over you. As you go about your work today, the eyes of the Lord are watching over you.

Your Creator watches over you. He who laid out every moment of your life before you were born, has blessed you with the intelligence and abilities to navigate each life experience. God watches over you with a heart of tender compassion filled with love for you, just as a mother watches over her children. God watches over you, longing for you to know and experience his great love today.

If your faith wavers today, remember that God is watching over you so that he can strengthen you. He knows that you live in a fallen world. He knows your weaknesses and where you may stumble and fall. When you are tempted today to rely on your own resources and abilities, remember that God is watching over you, ready to do exceedingly more than you can ask, imagine, or do in your own strength.

God knows when Satan is or will be tempting you. Satan has

only the power that God permits. When Satan asked to tempt the disciples, Jesus prayed that their faith would not fail. In the same way, God's eyes are upon you, not to see your faith fail, but to strengthen you so that your faith will not fail.

> Turn from evil and do good; seek peace and pursue it.
>
> The eyes of the Lord are on the righteous, and his ears are attentive to their cry; but the face of the Lord is against those who do evil, to blot out their name from the earth.
>
> The righteous cry out, and the Lord hears them; he delivers them from all their troubles. The Lord is close to the brokenhearted and saves those who are crushed in spirit.
>
> The righteous person may have many troubles, but the Lord delivers him from them all; he protects all his bones, not one of them will be broken. (Psalm 34:14–20)

PRAYER

Almighty God, thank you for watching over me. Thank you for loving me. Lord, you know my weaknesses. Strengthen me today so that I can stand firm. Lead me not into temptation. For yours is the kingdom and the power and the glory forever and ever. *Amen.*

DAY 21

Why Are You Afraid?

When I am afraid, I put my trust in you.
In God, whose word I praise—
in God I trust and am not afraid.
What can mere mortals do to me?

PSALM 56:3-4

When you're afraid, is God trustworthy?

We were sitting on the eleventh floor in the middle of a lunchtime Bible study. Suddenly the fire alarm went off. It was a loud, annoying, persistent beeping. After a few minutes, a voice came over the speaker: "An alarm condition exists elsewhere in the complex that is being investigated."

The beeps continued. We wondered if we were in danger. Could we trust the person investigating to warn us in time if we had to evacuate?

Fear is something like a fire alarm. You hear a rumor and wonder if you are in danger. Or maybe you work for somebody who believes fear is the best way to motivate employees to conform to the corporate expectations, so you are constantly looking over your shoulder, wondering if your performance is acceptable.

The Bible teaches us that you don't have to fear people—for

they cannot harm you. The Lord is your refuge. No matter what happens to you and regardless of your circumstances, nothing can separate you from God's love. His love and acceptance are not dependent on your successes or failures. God's love for you has not changed and will not change. When you rest in the knowledge that your faith is secure, you have the peace, strength, and courage to live out your convictions. Resting on the truth that God keeps his covenant of loyal love with those who love him and observe his commandments (Deut. 7:9), you can go about your work with a smile on your face and peace in your heart.

God chose you because he loves you. He loves you because he loves you. And that's that!

What courageous decision do you need to make, whom do you need to speak to, what do you need to stop doing, or what next step must you take to stand firm in Christ's love in your place of work?

PRAYER

Almighty God, you see my troubles, hardships, persecutions, famines, dangers, and nakedness. Yet I thank you that through the death and resurrection of your Son, I am more than conqueror. Fill me with your peace and joy at work. *Amen.*

DAY 22

God's Presence

Where can I go from your Spirit?
Where can I flee from your presence?
PSALM 139:7

The real beauty of the incarnation is that Christ left his home in heaven, became a man, and came to earth—all for humanity's benefit. He came for every hard or happy day you will ever face. He promised to be near you every moment, even when your work is enjoyable and fulfilling and you look forward every morning to going to work. God is with you when your work is dry and boring and it is an effort just to get out of bed. God is with you when you are promoted and receive increased responsibilities, or when you are demoted.

God is present in the middle of both the satisfaction and stress of work. God's hand is always upon you—at work, at home, or wherever you are! God is fully aware of every one of your anxieties. He searches you and knows your heart. You don't need to be afraid!

God is aware of your thoughts about your coworkers, managers, and job. He knows what you are going to say even before you say it. He is with you in your meetings, when you're dealing with customers, at the water cooler, and in the lunch room. Even in your darkest place, God's light shines brightly!

God's Presence

When you reflect on God's awareness of everything you say, think, and do at work, know that he accepts you just as you are. He is gracious and freely offers forgiveness without condemning you. You are not alone!

PRAYER

Heavenly Father, I am humbled and amazed that you know me completely. Forgive me for those things I have thought, said, or done that I shouldn't have. I praise you that I am not alone at work today, but that you are there with me in every activity, meeting, and interaction with others at work. Thank you that your light shines brightly in my workplace. *Amen.*

DAY 23

Working with Integrity

*The fruit of the righteous is a tree of life,
and the one who is wise saves lives.*

PROVERBS 11:30

Throughout your day, you make thousands of small decisions about how you live. Do you choose to cheat in some small way, or do you maintain integrity in everything you do? Are your behavior and attitudes motivated by pride or by humility? Are you faithful in your relationships with coworkers? Do you pursue wealth at all costs, or do you pursue righteousness? Do people at work know you for your blameless, impeccable character? Do you place your hope in other people, or do you fully hope in God? What about your speech? Can you be trusted to keep secrets and hold your tongue, or are you known as the office gossip? Do people say you are ruthless, cruel, deceptive, or a back stabber? Or do they refer to you as kindhearted and desiring good things for your coworkers and company? Do others recognize you for your generosity with your time and abilities?

Through the power of the Holy Spirit you can live a life of integrity, refusing to be tempted to use the world's methods of "getting ahead." Thanks be to God, it is possible to escape the temptations of your workplace and to resist the devil. Yes, Jesus understands your temptations, for he was tempted in every way we are, yet he did not sin. In fact God will not let you be tempted beyond what you can bear. And when you are tempted, God will provide a way out so that you can endure it (1 Cor. 10:13).

Because Jesus is alive, you can choose to work with integrity, humbly pursuing righteousness with your hope firmly placed in God. May you be known as one who holds your tongue. Honor your employer and coworkers by being kind-hearted and generous, spreading seeds of righteousness and seeking the good of your coworkers and employer.

Then you will know the favor of the Lord. Your path will be straight, even when facing difficult choices. You will be like a tree planted by streams of water, yielding fruit in season and bringing shade and beauty where you live and work.

PRAYER

Almighty God, I know that you understand the temptations I face today. I ask for your mercy and grace to help me in my time of need. Don't let me yield to temptation but rescue me from the Evil One. For yours is the kingdom and the power and the glory forever. *Amen.*

DAY 24

An Oasis of Grace

*Finally, all of you, be like-minded,
be sympathetic, love one another,
be compassionate and humble.*
1 Peter 3:8

Imagine your work area as a sacred space, an oasis of grace. A place where everybody shows sincere love for one another. Where gentleness exists and mutual respect for each person's talents and skills is appreciated. Where people submit to their managers or employers for the Lord's sake. Imagine an organization where people are tenderhearted and humble. Where empathy flows freely. Where insults are repaid with blessings.

Envision a culture of peace marked by open, honest conversations, where coworkers focus on what is true, honorable, right, pure, loving, and admirable. Imagine a workplace in which you are respected for the skills and talents God blessed you with, and where you have opportunities to flourish and make meaningful contributions.

What thoughts are going through your mind as you picture this workplace? What would the conversations be like in this workplace? What would happen when you make a mistake, or you can't quite figure out how to do your job? What would people say to you when you come to work carrying the

An Oasis of Grace

joys and burdens of life? Would getting up this morning have been easier if this describes your work environment?

Although this may not be a picture of your work environment, are glimmers of any of these attributes there? Which of these characteristics do you see in your workplace, albeit imperfectly? Take a moment to praise the Lord for these.

Our Lord Jesus, when he walked the earth, created sacred spaces of grace in every interaction he had with people. He pours out his grace on us, he builds us up together into a spiritual temple and a holy priesthood, so together we can create sacred spaces, oases of grace.

How could you live your life, with family, friends, and coworkers, to create a sacred space, an oasis of grace, for others in your sphere of influence?

PRAYER

Almighty God, thank you that your eyes are on the righteous and your ears are attentive to their cry. Grant me the courage and wisdom to create an oasis of grace where I live and work. *Amen.*

DAY 25

The Way of Righteousness

*In the way of righteousness there is life;
along that path is immortality.*
PROVERBS 12:28

To enter the way of righteousness, you must believe that Jesus died for your sins. For only then are you able to stand righteous in God's presence. When you walk along the way of righteousness, your circumstances may not change, but the way you experience them will change, for God walks beside you.

One of the joys of walking the way of righteousness is knowing that you're exactly where you're supposed to be. God gave you exactly the right mind, talents, and skills to perform every job assigned to you with reverence for the Lord (Eph. 6:5–8; Col. 3:22–25). Walking the way of righteousness gives you the freedom, without false pretenses, to be the wonderful person God created you to be.

As you walk the way of righteousness, "if it is possible, so far as it depends on you, live at peace with everyone" (Rom. 12:18). Choose your words carefully to bring joy, healing, and peace. Use words that are faithful and true, gentle and kind, uplifting and encouraging.

The Way of Righteousness

Sometimes you may find yourself working in a hostile environment. The way of righteousness does not always remove you from these situations but instead takes you through them. With God at your side, you can experience abundant life even when your manager reigns with fear and intimidation, or coworkers make life miserable, or your Christian values are mocked or not tolerated.

The way of righteousness is not about being at peace with all people but possessing peace with God. God's sight pierces the secrets of every soul. When schemers surround you, trust the Lord to keep you and your family safe. When your coworkers are ungrateful, liars, or fantasy chasers, be known as one who is trustworthy. The way of righteousness is an invitation to walk by faith and to "act justly and love mercy" (Micah 6:8).

As you walk the way of righteousness, God is constantly working in your life through his Word to make you more like Christ. By demonstrating the fruit of the Spirit and the virtues of Christ, who called you out of darkness into his marvelous light, you reflect God's glory. If people praise you for your prudence, quietly acknowledge God as the source of your wisdom.

At the end of the way of righteousness you will see your Savior with a big smile across his face and arms outstretched to welcome you into heaven. Then you will hear him say, "My child, well done good and faithful servant!"

PRAYER

Almighty God, as I walk along the way of righteousness, may you receive all the glory and honor for the choices I make and the way I behave. *Amen.*

DAY 26

Courage

> *Have I not commanded you? Be strong and courageous.*
> *Do not be afraid; do not be discouraged, for the Lord*
> *your God will be with you wherever you go.*
>
> JOSHUA 1:9

How do you find the strength and courage to face your daily work routines? Where do you find the courage to step out into a new career or a new position?

God is sufficient to replace your anxieties, inadequacies, fears, and doubts with courage and confidence.

It would be nice if God provided a twelve-step program to courage, or seven habits for courageous living. However, he gave something much more amazing: his promises, found in his Word and his presence.

Your strength and courage rests in God. He is the supernatural power who created this world and acted throughout history and in your life. All power on heaven and earth belongs to God. Because he is unchanging, his power will continue to act today, tomorrow, and for all tomorrows. God's promises are dependable because they rest entirely on his unchanging character. Nothing that God promises or does relies on you or anybody else.

God reveals himself to you in the Bible so that you can grasp the length and breadth and height and depth of his love for you. He shows you how to live in a right relationship with him so that he can provide the strength you need for today and tomorrow.

Daily hear what God says about you and to you through his Word. Don't be distracted by inferiority-complex podcasts from your youth, fear-mongering messages from well-intentioned friends, or people comparing you with your predecessor.

The wisdom you need today to move forward with courage and confidence can only be discovered in the Bible. Knowing what God says to you in the Bible requires consistent lifelong

- meditation on God's Word to make it part of your normal, day-to-day reasoning and thinking;
- exploring with other believers how the truths of God's Word apply to everyday situations;
- making God's Word part of your everyday conversations; and
- being able to explain how God's Word influences your day-to-day actions and larger decisions.

You may know a lot about God's promises, about the Bible, about yourself, and that God is with you, but true courage will not come until you step out in faith and obey his Word. Obedience may mean faithfully doing exactly what you were doing yesterday and the day before. Obedience may mean dealing with sin in your life before you move forward. Obedience may mean holding God's hand as you take a leap of faith into something new.

"Be strong and very courageous. Be careful to obey all the law my servant Moses gave you; do not turn from it to the right or to the left, that you may be successful wherever you go" (Joshua 1:7).

PRAYER

Almighty God, I thank you that you are the fountain of wisdom. Grant me today the wisdom I need in every conversation and for every decision I need to make, so that I may live courageously and that your name be glorified. *Amen.*

DAY 27

Stewards of God's Creation

*God blessed them and said to them,
"Be fruitful and increase in number; fill the earth
and subdue it. Rule over the fish in the sea
and the birds in the sky and over every living creature
that moves on the ground."*

GENESIS 1:28

What command in Scripture were you obeying this morning when you went to work?

When you get up in the morning and go to work, you are heading out in obedience to God's command in Genesis 1:28 to fill the earth, subdue the earth, and rule over it. In other words, every job, every task, and every good endeavor you do today, you are doing in obedience to God's command to govern and be responsible for his creation.

When God created the world, he said his work "was good." He worked for the sheer joy of working. Our universe is a masterpiece designed by a master craftsman and artist—God.

When God created the world, he created it for you and me, and he created us to be stewards of his world. As God's vice-regents, through our work we have the privilege of entering into the story of

God's creative work. He created this world so that at a macro level it would survive for millennia. At the micro level, God designed the world to require our continual stewardship.

Starting with Adam, God gave him a garden in a corner of creation, with water and animals and everything necessary for him to tend the garden. Work was part of God's blessing, God's goodness, and the environment of the garden. By working in this garden, Adam provided for himself and his family.

From that garden subsequent generations built the great pyramids in Egypt. Later the Greek and Roman cultures arose. From that garden, we now have airplanes, trains, cars, medicine, the Internet, McDonald's, and Starbucks. At the dawn of creation, God foresaw each unique way that humanity would fill the earth, subdue it, and rule over it (Gen. 1:28). It is the work of societies and cultures to help people thrive and flourish in God's creation.

Before the dawn of creation, God prepared unique good works just for you to do (Eph. 2:10). God created you to be responsible to develop, care for, enrich, explore, cultivate, and govern the corner of the world where you live. He expects and encourages you to maximize creation's full potential through your work.

PRAYER

> Almighty God, I praise you for the opportunity you have given me to work in this wonderful world you created. Help me to do my job today with excellence so that your world may continue to flourish. *Amen.*

DAY 28

No Little Tasks

God saw all that he had made, and it was very good.
GENESIS 1:31

God wired work into our DNA. We need work to grow physically, emotionally, and spiritually. Work is part of the blessing and the goodness of God's creation. When we work, we are reflecting God's image and character.

God used his mind, knowledge, and wisdom to shape every aspect of the universe. Then he blessed us with minds that can seek out the ways his world works and the ways of God in his world.

God strategically created the world. He didn't create the animals first and then wonder where to put them. He had everything planned. When you develop strategies for your work, you reflect God's perfect planning.

Everything God created is unique. Consider the beauty of a flower or the variety of flavors of food. God trusts you to reflect his creativity in everything you make.

As God created the universe, he named the light "day" and the darkness "night." He calls each star by name. He gave us the privilege to name each animal, bird, and plant and to name our children. Like God, when you name something, you give it the dignity God intended it to have while describing its character.

God took the earth, which was formless and empty, and shaped it into this world we enjoy, including all its processes, systems, and natural laws. When we present data in a spreadsheet, or mix ingredients to serve a delicious meal, or lead people to finish a project in a structured and orderly fashion, we mirror the enjoyment God takes in his creation.

God cares for each one of us. Each hair on your head is numbered. He knows your name. He cares for every aspect of his creation. Not one sparrow falls or flower dies without his knowing. When you care for or demonstrate compassion for others, you model God's compassion and care.

On the seventh day, God rested from his work. Rest … knowing your work is good. Rest … trusting that God will take care of you and your work.

There are no little tasks in God's kingdom, for each one has equal value in God's eyes. Each task is needed for somebody to flourish. Each task is necessary for people to enjoy God's creation. Each task is essential to obey God's command to rule over and subdue the earth.

PRAYER

Almighty God, you entrusted me with my job. Help me to do my job in such a way that it reflects your image and character. *Amen.*

DAY 29

Can God Fix It?

*But because of his great love for us, God,
who is rich in mercy, made us alive with Christ
even when we were dead in transgressions—
it is by grace you have been saved.*

Ephesians 2:4–5

Have you ever shaken your head in dismay at your workplace's systems or processes? Have you ever watched people make decisions that protect only their own interests? Have you ever been frustrated that work is not going the way you want it to?

If somebody were to sit down with you and ask you to list three problems with your workplace, how long would you have to think before you could respond? If you ask questions like "Can God resolve these problems?" or "Will God fix them the way we want them fixed?" you run the risk of doubting God's Word, as Adam and Eve did.

Every aspect of Adam's work in the garden was enjoyable. He got up every morning and together with his wife, Eve, they performed the work God called them to do.

Suddenly a workplace disaster of cosmic proportions occurred.

Satan commissioned Pride, disguised as a serpent, to interrupt Adam and Eve in their work. Satan's words were enticing,

"You will be like God." Pride's twin sister, Shame, lurking in the shadows, watched with glee as Adam and Eve put aside their work, doubted God's Word, and succumbed to temptation. Sin entered into God's perfect creation.

Everything changed in that moment. Yet nobody stopped breathing. The earth didn't stop turning or orbiting the sun. But the consequences of sin, of not trusting God, started to ripple throughout the world.

From that moment when sin entered creation, all work became hampered by pain, thorns, and thistles. Frustration, dissatisfaction, and fruitlessness marred all work. Apart from God, work became a means to find identity and self-worth. Unity and love was replaced with deceit, blame, manipulation, comparison, competition, disunity, and strife. Work and God's creation became a means to satisfying personal desires, controlling one's destiny, and accumulating power.

Could anything be done to remediate this catastrophic, cataclysmic event?

This dire situation wasn't beyond redemption! God didn't pull out a contingency plan to try to mitigate the damage. He didn't invoke the angelic emergency response team. Because of his sovereignty, he remained completely in control.

By his grace God gave Adam and Eve the privilege to continue to be participants in his story. By his grace God continued to allow his creation to be fruitful and multiply, although it would be painful. By his grace God continued to offer provision for the physical needs for existence, although thorns and thistles would make life more difficult. By his grace God offered provision for the emotional needs for survival as he clothed Adam and Eve, covering their shame and nakedness.

By his grace God offers provision for the spiritual needs for survival through the death and resurrection of his son, Jesus. By his grace God delivers hope for a future workplace in a new heaven and a new earth untainted by sin. By his grace God makes available a path to unity with him and with others.

By his mercy God allows each person to accept or reject his grace.

This isn't the storyline that Adam and Eve expected. Nor is it the storyline that anybody anticipated. This is God's story!

This is a story the angels watch with bated breath (1 Peter 1:10–12; 1 Tim. 3:16). This story of grace is a tale of redemption that is playing out today in the world and in your workplace. Your workplace is part of God's story. By his grace God is weaving your workplace into his story. Since you aren't the author of the story of your workplace, this story won't unfold the way you expect, but it will unfold in accordance with God's grace.

If God can take the worst cataclysmic event in history and turn it into a story of redemption, what could God do in your workplace?

PRAYER

Almighty God, I thank you that you are aware of everything that is happening at my workplace. Help me to trust you to weave the drama of my workplace into your story of grace and redemption. *Amen.*

DAY 30

Thriving in Your Workplace

*Seek the peace and prosperity of the city
to which I have carried you into exile.
Pray to the Lord for it, because if it prospers,
you too will prosper.*

JEREMIAH 29:7

As a Christian, you can thrive in your job. You can perform your work with strength, confidence, courage, and excellence, knowing that God loves you. You can be faithful to God and loyal to your employer even when situations arise at work that are inconsistent with biblical values, such as truth, honor, integrity, and honesty. You can seek the good of the people you work with as well as the good of your employer.

You can live with integrity while wisely taking advantage of each opportunity for personal advancement. You can boldly embrace every opportunity God presents to you to influence the culture of your organization. You can lead in such a way that people will rejoice in your leadership (Prov. 11:10).

Many dangers and risks to your walk of faith are found in the workplace. Discernment isn't always easy. Pride or discouragement threaten to destabilize you. You may be tempted by the lie that you are unworthy and incapable, or selfish ambition might tempt you to act foolishly. Therefore, God provides wise mentors and leaders (not all of whom may be Christian) to speak wisdom, to encourage you to step out in faith at the right time, and to help you see your blind spots. God provides his Word to guide you into all truth.

Work doesn't always go well. Your actions of loyalty or pursuit of the welfare and success of the department or company may not always be recognized. However, as a Christian your motivation is not in being recognized by the world but in glorifying God. When you live to please God, when you choose to do each task with excellence, God may choose to exalt you . . . or he may not. His purposes are beyond your comprehension.

Don't fret when you see haughty eyes, hear lying tongues, discern hearts that devise wicked schemes, and watch people rushing into evil. Don't be disturbed when false witnesses or persons stir up conflict surround you. The Lord hates all of these (Prov. 6:16–19). God has proven throughout history that he is more than capable of dealing with these situations in his own way at his own time. Humbly ask God to accomplish his divine purposes in the midst of your workplace.

God works through your kindness, graciousness, loyalty, courage, ingenuity, and diplomacy. With the craft and courage of Christian leaders, divinely inspired coincidences can change the trajectory of organizations. Without God's timely intervention, all the wisdom of the world will not bring success. Prayerfully and patiently wait for strategic events controlled by God to bring a climax to the drama of your workplace.

When you adhere to biblical values and wisdom, when you allow your godly character to speak more than your words, you will gain the favor of your colleagues. Through grace-filled living, you will be known as a person of wisdom and righteousness in your workplace.

PRAYER

Almighty God, you are sovereign over every aspect of this world, and you are sovereign over my workplace. Through your grace help me to be a person known for wisdom and righteousness in my company so that your name may be glorified. *Amen.*

DAY 31

Abiding in Christ in the Workplace

*Whoever confesses that Jesus is the Son of God,
God abides in him, and he in God.*
1 JOHN 4:15 (NKJV)

Jesus invites you today to continue to abide in him. He desires you to abide in him in every task you do, as you respond to emails, make phone calls, and in every interaction with customers and colleagues. Every one of your needs will be met when you abide in Christ, for he is sufficient.

Every place you sit, stand, or walk past is where God loves you. Everything you do is done in a place where God loves you and where God is present.

Jesus chose you and invites you to maintain your friendship with him every moment of every day. This is an invitation to intimate fellowship in which you are fully known and fully loved. It is an open invitation to boldly come to your Father in heaven with your prayers, knowing that God is delighted to hear your voice and to answer your requests.

Abiding in Christ is all about your relationship with God. Abiding in Christ has nothing to do with your work. You can abide in Christ when you are working for the greatest boss in the world, when you are working for the boss who reigns with fear, or working for a boss who manipulates people or stretches the truth. You can abide in Christ when you feel like a square peg in a round hole, or when you thoroughly enjoy your work. You can abide in Christ whether work keeps you crazy busy or you've been laid off.

Esther and Mordecai lived in a foreign land, among people who did not believe in God. Both knew the secret of abiding in God. After reporting a plot on the king's life but not receiving recognition or thanks for many years, Mordecai continued to faithfully do his job without griping because he abided in God (Esther 2:19–23). Because she abided in God, Esther could live in the king's harem along with all the other virgins waiting to learn who the king would choose as his queen (vv. 1–17).

Abiding in Christ is not assurance that life will go smoothly. We live in a fallen world and with all the effects of the fall. When we abide in Christ, we don't walk through this world alone; yet this is not an assurance that we won't be persecuted for our faith. In fact, just as two magnets repel each other, you may find that some people find you repulsive because of your life in Christ. As Esther and Mordecai experienced, some people, like Haman, considered them and all the Jews repulsive. Not only did Haman find the Jews repulsive, he went out of his way to exterminate them all (Esther 3). Esther's courage to patiently speak at the right time with a gentle tongue came from abiding in God (Esther 4—7; Prov. 25:15).

When you are abiding in Christ, you are presenting the Lord as holy in the sight of the people you work with. When you do your work as an outflow of abiding with Christ, you will be a blessing to the people you work with, and they will hold you in high esteem (Esther 10:3; Prov. 11:10).

Not abiding in Christ not only impacts your life but also ripples through the lives of the people you work with. Moses learned this the hard way when he struck the rock instead of speaking to it (Num. 20:11–13). Each person is accountable before God for how, or if, they abide in Christ.

All humans have an innate desire for fruitfulness. But to be fruitful, you must be connected to the source of nourishment—Christ, your Creator and the Creator of this universe. When you abide in Christ, you will bear fruit according to the gifts and skills God blessed you with. When you abide in Christ, your work will be pleasing in the eyes of your Father.

When you abide in Christ, you will be filled with an inexplicable joy that is not defined by how your work is going or by the people you work with. Heavenly joy is not deterred by suffering or circumstances.

In each task you do today, in the place where you find yourself right now, abide in God's Word. Allow Christ to transform your heart through his Word. In each email and conversation abide in God's love. Allow Christ to fill your heart with love for all people. Then watch God weave together your life's story to surprise you with joy as he accomplishes his divine purpose.

Remember, God loves you and has chosen you! Abide in him!

PRAYER

Almighty God, thank you that you have raised me up in Christ and seated me in the heavenly realms in Christ Jesus. Help me to abide in you as I go about my work in order that my life might reflect the incomparable riches of your grace. *Amen.*

About the Author

James Bruyn (BMath, MATS, CMA, PMP) is a bi-vocational visionary leader, writer, and speaker who enjoys helping individuals integrate their faith in God with their daily life. James is passionate about connecting the rich promises of our loving heavenly Father with the joys and challenges of living out our faith in the workplace. He currently works as a consultant for the rail industry, as well as authoring Marketplace Bible Studies, leading Marketplace Ministry in Calgary, Alberta, and providing leadership coaching.

James has been involved in many aspects of ministry leadership, including church planting, young adult ministry, preaching, and board leadership for churches and the Navigators of Canada. He and his wife, Susan, have three adult children.

Visit the author at **www.marketplace-ministry.ca**.

Also by the Author

MARKETPLACE BIBLE STUDIES 1
GOD WITH US AT WORK

Does your faith in Christ change the way you go about your work?

As Christians working in the marketplace, we're surrounded by competing ideas that often conflict with our Christian values and beliefs. We may work in environments where loving God with all our heart, soul, and mind is a foreign concept. How do we find joy and peace when our beliefs may not be understood or encouraged? How do we demonstrate the love of God to our coworkers and customers?

These studies offer a guide to explore how Scripture relates to your work experiences and what God has to say about your vocation and your coworkers. Take some time over a coffee break or lunch to embark on this journey of discovery with your coworkers or friends.

MARKETPLACE BIBLE STUDIES 2
GIFTED TO DO OUR WORK

Has God prepared you to face your workday? Does it feel like the cost of working with integrity and standing firm in your faith is too high a price to pay? Is there any benefit to being identified as a Christian at work? And what does it mean to do all that you do in the name of Jesus? In the sequel to *God with Us at Work*, James Bruyn will help you delve deeper into your workplace attitudes and relationships to give you practical ways to approach your daily work. This book will help you to see how you can use your God-given gifts at work and how to do the will of God as you go about your job.

Your workplace is an excellent place to see God working in your life. So take some time over a coffee break or lunch to embark on this journey of discovery with your coworkers or friends.

www.ingramcontent.com/pod-product-compliance
Lightning Source LLC
Chambersburg PA
CBHW072208100526
44589CB00015B/2423